Contents

Introduction

The Well. 18

Map 20

Wells 21

    Lewis 21

    Harris 42

    North Uist 47

    Benbecula 55

    South Uist 58

    Barra 64

    St. Kilda 75

Bibliography 82

Notes 84

First published in Scotland in 2000
by Acair Ltd., 7 James Street,
Stornoway, Isle of Lewis.
Tel: 01851 703020
Fax: 01851 703294
e-mail: acair@virginbiz.com
www.acairbooks.com

All rights reserved.
No part of this publication may be reproduced
in any form or by any means without the prior
written permission of Acair Ltd.

© 2000 Text Finlay Macleod
© 2000 Photographs Donald John Campbell

Designed and typeset by Acair Ltd.
Text and cover design Margaret Anne MacLeod

Printed by ColourBooks, Dublin

ISBN 0 86152 266 4

The Healing Wells
of the Western Isles

Finlay MacLeod

photographs
Donald John Campbell

acair

Introduction

People have always been mindful of water for it is at the heart of all living matter. It is therefore no surprise that it has been viewed as a resource with powerful properties, and as something to which mankind has strong attachment. Consequently importance was attached to locations which held water - such as lochs, rivers and wells or springs. These locations nearly always emanate a sense of beauty, but people have been aware that they are also special places, and in a sense people viewed them as living locations - alive with their own particular spirit, as were many other phenomena in their world.

People have therefore come to associate wells with strength and succour, believing that they would receive assistance, information and advice from them. But in order to receive this, they had to approach the wells in a particular way, and they had to adhere closely to associated customs. If they did not do so, the live spirit of the well would not be able to assist them.

Banks (1937) wrote: "Wells, springs, streams and pools have been accredited with healing powers, wherever man has had ailments to cure, and Scotland with its numerous mountains and glens was famed more than many other lands for healing waters. Long before the Christian era, springs endowed with magical virtue were regarded as bringers of health from the heart of the earth." (125).

It is rather difficult for us nowadays to imagine ourselves in these situations, and to understand how people perceived their world and its mode of operation. Nobody nowadays ascribes a living power to the physical environment as was the case in times past. As a result, neither wells nor such special places hold any potency for them, and these sites cease to be meaningful and are forgotten about.

But this was not always the case. Many hundreds of wells were located throughout the country and it is estimated that there were at least six hundred healing wells throughout Scotland - with people being very much aware of them and affording them high status. Many of these wells were named after different saints such as St Columba, St Andrew, St Ronan and many others. Linked with Christianity there were also many small chapels in differing locations and sometimes wells were associated with these chapels (See MacLeod, 1997). This illustrates how the people viewed the wells as spiritual sanctuaries which were closely linked to the chapels. The wells served as a visible part of how people imposed a pattern on the world in which they lived and of the spiritual sense which guided their understanding of that world.

As part of their beliefs the daily lives of the people were heavily influenced by oral tradition. They expressed their philosophy through that oral tradition, and as expected, water and wells occupied their own place within that tradition, with many tales and traditions linked to some of these wells.

Different people have written accounts of the many customs connected with wells and the confidence that people had in them. Arthur Mitchell (1880) wrote: "The adoration of wells may be encountered in Scotland from John O' Groats to the Mull of Galloway. I have seen a dozen wells in Scotland that have not ceased to be worshipped. Nowadays, the visitors are are comparatively few, and those who go are generally in earnest. The object is usually the restoration to health of some poor little child. Indeed the cure of sick children is a special virtue of many of these wells." And JF Campbell wrote in Popular Tales of the West Highlands (1892): "Holy healing wells are common all over the Highlands; and people still leave offerings of pins and nails and bits of rag, though few would confess it. There is a well in Islay where I myself have, after drinking, deposited copper caps amongst a hoard of pins and buttons and similar gear placed in chinks in the rocks and trees at the edge of the 'Witches' Well'." (2, 145).

There were wells located throughout the Western Isles often with specific names, and with information and customs associated with them. Although this knowledge has withered over the years, a good deal of it still remains, and it is this knowledge which this small book seeks to bring together. There is not the same interest now in wells as once existed; people's views on such topics have greatly altered. People nowadays do not have the same vision of the world as was once prevalent and because of this the detailed knowledge of places and wells which once existed is no more. Despite that, wells are still to be found in the Western Isles with associated tales which give an example of the beliefs which were common about wells throughout the country.

For example it was said that it was offensive to the spirit of the well if that spirit were insulted in any way. The well could move on account of it or close up. Oral tradition has it that Tobar Thòmais in

Geàrrannan could move if a cow were to excrete too close to it, and the spirit of Tobar Thiobartan moved because a man took his one-eyed horse there for a cure. Martin Martin has a particular account of a well in Colonsay which fled to Islay: "A mile on the south-west side of the cave Uah Vearnag is the celebrated well called Toubir-in-Knahar, which, in the ancient language, is as much as to say the well has sailed from one place to another; for it is a received tradition of the vulgar inhabitants of this isle, and the opposite isle of Colonsay, that this well was first in Colonsay, until an imputent woman happened to wash her hands in it, and that immediately after, the well being thus abused, came in an instant to Islay, where it is like to continue, and is ever since esteemed a catholicon for diseases by the natives and adjacent islanders, and the great resort to it is commonly every quarter-day. It is common with sick people to make a vow to come to the well, and after drinking it they make a tour sunways round it, and then leave an offering of some small token, such as a pin, needle, farthing, or the like, on the stone cover which is above the well. But if the patient is now like to recover they send of the water to be drunk by the sick person. There is a little chapel beside the well, to which such as had found the benefit of the water, came back and returned thanks to God for their recovery." (274).

By the same token, a dog must not drink from one of the wells in Uamh Uladal, or it would dry up as a result. It was said that some wells had an ability to foretell the future: the most notable well with such properties in the Western Isles being Tobar Anndrais in Siadar, which could give an indication whether patients would survive their illness. Also some people verified their love vows at wells or requested that they should enjoy good luck - Tobar Chaluim Chille in Tangasdal was one such well.

Other singular accounts were given of wells - one which would not whiten linen, and one whose water could not be boiled. Some others carried the name of 'tobar nam buadh' or well of virtues and there are two such wells in the Western Isles - one in Kismul Castle and a particularly notable one in St Kilda. The Gaels referred to delicious water by using the word 'wine' and there is one well called 'tobar creag an fhìon' (well of the wine rock) in the Western Isles, in South Uist.

Some wells commanded great respect because of their curative powers for the treatment of mental illness. On mainland Scotland, two wells in particular are associated with such curative powers. These are

Tobar Mhaolruibhe on the island of Maolruibhe and the spa at St Fillans. In an early account of Tobar Mhaolruibhe Pennant (1774) states: "The curiosity of the place is the well of the saint; of power unspeakable in cases of lunacy." (330). Each person suffering from mental illness who sought a cure at the well drank from it and stuck coins in a tree beside the well, and the patient had then to be dragged round the island tied to a boat. Arthur Mitchell who visited the well in 1880 wrote: "One of the things which the Presbytery of Dingwall (in mid-17th Century) deplored and sought to suppress was the adoration of wells. Now, in certain aspects, this adoration of wells continues largely to our day. Even the very well on Innis Maree, which the Dingwall Presbytery had prominently in view at their meeting on the 5th of September 1656, still receives adoration. When I visited it some fifteen years ago, I found numerous offerings fastened to the tree which stands beside it." (149).

The well has now dried up but people still stick coins in the surrounding trees. It was only once a year that patients suffering from mental illness were taken to the St Fillans waters to seek a cure.

The water in Tobar Chùisdein in Point falls into the sea, and oral tradition (and Martin Martin) relates that patients with mental illness found relief if they stood for a while under the stream falling from the well. People travelled long distances to seek relief. But the best account available of this phenomenon is in connection with Tobar an Teampaill/Tobar Rònain and Teampall Mholuaidh in Eòrapaidh. Oral tradition in Ness has been strong in giving an account of activities surrounding the chapel and the well. Martin Martin collected information about these customs. The patient was brought to this place and he had to drink and be baptised with the water from the well, and he had to go sunwise round the chapel and spend the night bound beside the altar, and his chances of recovery were higher if he were able to sleep. Many other stories about this site are still in existence: in ancient times in Ness this location was a prime revelation of the mysterious world which the people inhabited.

Well water was also thought to be a cure for epilepsy. But there was an added element connected with this: and that was a human skull. A visit was made to the graveyard during the hours of darkness where a skull was dug up and brought home. Water was then taken from a healing well and the patient drank the water from the skull. The skull had to be returned that same night. People were generally of the opinon that the skull of someone who had taken their own life was the most effective. A tale similar to this was told in Borgh, Lewis. Anne Ross (1966) wrote: "The skull of a suicide, often filled with water from a holy well, was a known and much-believed-in cure for epilepsy, but it was held in reserve as a final measure, when all other, less dramatic remedies had failed. In Lewis, the skull of an ancestor would be dug up from a special place in the graveyard, after sunset and before sunrise, and water placed in it from a sacred well; this was then taken to the patient and he or she had to drink it, the whole ritual, from beginning to end, being performed in silence." (80-81).

The Rev. William Matheson gave the following account to Anne Ross (1962) in connection with skulls and wells: "A similar tradition was still current in comparatively recent years in the island of Lewis. An elder of the United Free Church in Ness had an epileptic daughter. He eventually decided to try to cure her of epilepsy in a traditional manner. Between sunset and sunrise and without speaking to a living thing, he walked five miles to the family burial-ground at Teampull Chrò Naoimh at North (sic) Galson. There he dug up the grave and removed the skull from it. He came back home with the skull, awakened the epileptic girl and made her drink from the skull. He then walked back to Teampull Chrò Naoimh to re-bury the skull. My informant did not know the name of the well from which the water was taken, but it is likely to have been a healing well and its name should still be ascertainable." (36-37). There is no definite evidence as to the location of the well referred to.

The Gaels believed that the human head had particular powers. In a manner of speaking they worshipped the head, and it often appeared in their art. It is not surprising therefore that they were of the opinion that a head would strenghthen the healing properties of a well, and as a consequence human heads were placed in wells. This custom dates very far back in the history of the Celts as a people. Anne Ross (1976) writes: "It was a powerful and ancient Celtic belief, of which there are many examples, that by placing a human head in a venerated well, the powers of the water - whatever they were, healing in general, effecting specific cures, imparting fertility, and so on - were markedly increased by the magic powers with which the human head was accredited in the Celtic world down the centuries." (81).

The one example that we know of in the Western Isles of 'tobar nan ceann' or well of the heads, is to be found in Barra, and Nan MacKinnon often spoke of it. It is noteworthy that this ancient Celtic belief is still to be found in the Western Isles down to the present day. Examples of 'tobar nan ceann' are to be found throughout Scotland.

It was also from Barra that the remarkable tale of cockles being found in a fresh water well originated and much has been written on the topic. There is no trace of this having arisen anywhere else other than in Barra except that Boece located his version in Mull: it seems as if this tale was passed from one writer to another.

There are one or two examples in the Western Isles of rain water being collected in hollows in stones - these are 'Tobar nan Cupan' and 'Tobar na Reulaig'. Cup-stones and receptacles in stone slabs are known to have been used to collect rain water for use as a cure for disease of the eyes and illnesses such as whooping-cough. Little is known of these remedies in the Western Isles today.

Most of the healing qualities of wells were associated with illness or toothache. There were many toothache wells throughout the Western Isles at one time, and a number are still known. Whether it was the coldness of the water which dulled the toothache or whether the walk to the well acted in a therapeutic way is not known. Whatever it was, the people believed that the water from these wells was effective in curing the pain of toothache. Very definite customs had been passed down showing them how to approach each particular well; very often it had to be early in the morning, before they had eaten, and they must not utter a word to another living person on their way to the well or on the way back. Some wells had their own associated customs as to how many mouthfuls of water should be consumed: for example, Tobar an Dèididh in Cnoc Ard in Ness, where seven mouthfuls had to be taken, with the first six being spurted back out on a stone but with the seventh one being swallowed.

Many wells were also visited to effect a cure for all sorts of aches, pains and illnesses, from a sore stomach to eye complaints and diabetes. There was also the belief of elderly people who were experiencing the loss of their energy and vigour: in their hospital bed and often on their death bed they craved for a cold mouthful of water from a healing well with which they had been acquainted in their childhood. Physicians often encouraged them to do this. Again we do not know whether these were cases of faith healing or whether minerals such as iron or sulphur in the water strengthened them while in their weak state. Many had a craving for a 'drink of the cold water' - water which was 'cold on a hot summer's day and warm on a cold winter's day', emanating from the depths of the earth.

Usually people had learnt that they ought to leave a token at the well if they were going to ask a favour. The act was everything - the value of the token was irrelevant.

There are at least two explanations as to why tokens were left beside the wells. It could have been a gift for the spirit of the well, giving thanks for the cure which the spirit had bestowed through the medium of the water, or that one had to make a gesture of payment before the spirit of the well would heal. But many believed that the patient was leaving a bit of himself there, as a symbol of the pain or ill health that he was leaving behind him. Probably both reasons were linked together, at least sometimes.

People felt they could leave any kind of items beside the well as an offering. It might seem to us that the little insignificant articles which were left have no meaning or sense; at times these were little stones or tufts of heather which they gathered on their way to the well.

Nowadays we tend to see bits of clothing hanging on trees close to some wells. That, or coins, where there are wishing wells. In the centre of the quadrangle of the university with which I myself am most acquainted, you can see many coins at the bottom of the well at examination time!

Through the wells we are able to see vestiges of customs which were at one time widespread throughout the land. Water was seen as a live and powerful element, and people were drawn to it although they were also in awe of it. The knowledge they had was knowledge of how they could attain health and wholesomeness through the power associated with water and wells. Although the nature of people's information has changed since those times, there are still remnants of ancient knowledge in existence, and some of the wells are still known, bearing witness to thought processes that are today not easy to penetrate.

The Well

Derick Thomson

Right in the village there's a little well
and the grass hides it,
green grass in sap closely thatching it.
I heard of it from an old woman
but she said: "The path is overgrown with bracken
where I often walked with my cogie,
and the cogie itself is warped."
When I looked in her lined face
I saw the bracken growing round the well of her eyes,
and hiding it from seeking and from desires,
and closing it, closing it.

"Nobody goes to that well now,"
said the old woman, "as we once went,
when we were young,
though its water is lovely and white."
And when I looked in her eyes through the bracken
I saw the sparkle of that water
that makes whole every hurt
till the hurt of the heart.

"And will you go there for me,"
said the old woman, "even with a thimble,
and bring me a drop of that hard water
that will bring colour to my cheeks."
I found the well at last,
and though her need was not the greatest
it was to her I brought the treasure.

It may be that the well
is something I saw in a dream,
for today when I went to seek it
I found only bracken and rushes,
and the old woman's eyes are closed
and a film has come over their merriment.

An Dealbh Briste, 1951.
(Creachadh na Clàrsaich, 1982)
(Translated by the author from the Gaelic original)

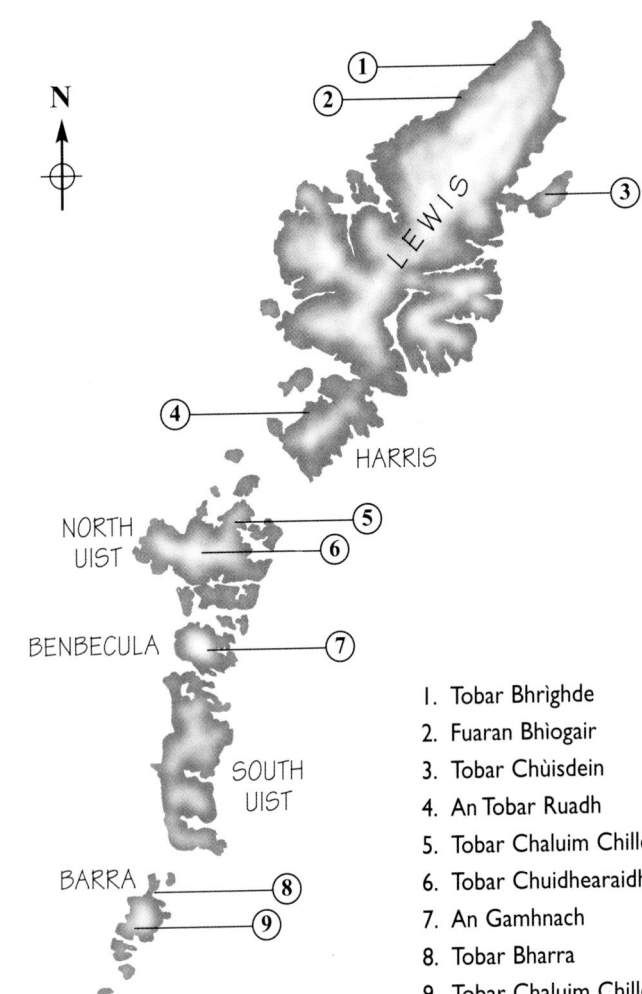

1. Tobar Bhrìghde
2. Fuaran Bhìogair
3. Tobar Chùisdein
4. An Tobar Ruadh
5. Tobar Chaluim Chille
6. Tobar Chuidhearaidh
7. An Gamhnach
8. Tobar Bharra
9. Tobar Chaluim Chille

~ *Lewis* ~

Fuaran Stoth NB 523659

This spring is to be found in Ness to the west of the road above Stoth bay, close to the Butt of Lewis. This well has iron properties and the local custom was for people to visit it in order to get a cure for stomach problems, as well as to generally get a feeling of wellbeing, having partaken of the water. It is not all that long since people gave up visiting this well.

Fuaran an Dèididh NB 535650

This spring is situated at Geodh nan Cruidh by the shore at Cnoc Ard, across from the north face of Dun Eistean. This was one of the toothache wells and people visited it to get relief from toothache. A person suffering from toothache would take seven mouthfuls from it and would spurt out six of these on a stone situated beside the well, but would drink the seventh mouthful.

MacPhail gives a different account: "At

Duneistein, near the Butt of Lewis, there is a well at the base of a high rock quite close to the sea, which goes by the name of 'Fuaran an dèididh', Toothache Well, and which is supposed to cure the toothache. The cure consists in taking in succession three mouthfuls of the water in this well, which are to be kept in one's mouth as long as convenient. Then each mouthful is to be spurted out on a large stone in a cave close at hand, on which the sun never shines. People afflicted with toothache still resort to Fuaran an dèididh for cure. The writer, in the sixties (1860s), was persuaded to do so." (MacPhail was from Shawbost: he was in Ness as a Gaelic teacher at that time.).

In the last few years the force of the sea has caused this well to close and has also caused the stone to disappear.

Tobar Rònain/Tobar an Teampaill
NB518649

This well is situated by the road in Eòrapaidh and the local people saw it as having a link with two chapels - St. Moluag's and St. Ronan's, both of which were close by.

At one time people suffering from mental illness were taken to St Moluag's. It was believed that people in this state would be cured if they slept for one night tied to the church altar. The person had to come to the church at nightfall and go round it sunwise seven times. The person then had to drink water from the well and had to also be baptised with water from it. The water was carried in a small receptacle, and that receptacle was in the custody of a family who were descendants of 'the clerks of the temple'.

This information has been handed down through tradition bearers and through the written word. Arthur Mitchell (1862), who was a lunacy inspector for the whole of Scotland wrote: "Lunatics are brought from many parts of the north-west of Scotland to this ruin. One man who had been taken there, and whom I saw, had the good fortune to sleep, and was cured. He afterwards married, and had a family. Seven years ago he again became insane, and

I found him labouring under dementia. I heard of several others in our own day, who had been sent to St Molonah - some from the mainland of Scotland - but no happy issue was reported. A Lewis gentleman, reading this paper in manuscript, writes on the margin: "I know two persons who were brought to the temple. The result was favourable, but one has had a return of the malady. It is said that a visit to the church has no efficacy for a return of the disease." (268). MacPhail was in Ness as a young teacher and he gives a particular account of the practice: "One of my earliest recollections in connection with the temple was one day, hearing people remarking that a young man, whose mind happened to be unhinged at the time, had been seen passing through the district in which I lived, in the custody of his friends, on his way to 'Teampull-Eoropie'. I was slightly acquainted thirty-five years ago with the individual in question. He was then quite sane."

Fuaran nam Maoim NB 556568

This spring is on the Ness moor. Two brothers from Lionel erected a cement covering for it. Murdo Maclean from Habost, Ness wrote: "A little bit further out from Gil Sgioba-Gearraidh was Airigh nam Maoim, and there was a spring there from which people used to drink, thinking it was good for this and that. It was full of iron.

Fuaran a' Ghròdhair NB 510637

This spring is beside the Swainbost river, inside the farmhouse wall, close to sands and machair land. People used to take water from it to treat toothache.

Tobar Chliamain NB 490624

This well was in North Dell, close to the site of Teampall Chliamain, south of Arnaistean. Nobody nowadays has any information on it, and nothing was written about it.

Tobar Bhrìghde NB 411574

This well is close to St Brigit's cemetery in Melbost, Borve. It is done up with cement, and people still use it. It has a narrow entrance but still wide enough to accommodate a small cup. The water in this well was effective in the treatment of jaundice.

Fuaran an Dèididh NB 4056

According to Peter Smith from Borve, this spring was to be found in at the shore on the croft closest to the Borve river, and to the west side of it. It was visited first thing in the morning and nobody must see the person actually visiting it. He said it was a small well.

Tobar Anndrais NB 384554

This is one of the most important wells in the Western Isles. It was Martin Martin who first described it: "St Andrew's well, in the village of Shader, is by the vulgar natives made a test to know if a sick person will die of the distemper he labours under. They send one with a wooden dish to bring some of the water to the patient, and if the dish, which is then laid softly upon the surface of the water, turn round sun-ways, they conclude that the patient will recover of that distemper; but if otherwise, that he will die." (90).

This once famous well is nowadays filled up with stones and a fence-post.

Fuaran an Dèididh NB 381554

This spring is down on the shore line north west of Teampall Pheadair. A nearby slope has long since fallen and concealed the well, which is no longer to be seen.

Tobar Mhoire NB 382550

This well is also known as Tobar Mhòr and/or Tobar Eire. It is at the roadside at Mol Eire. Although people are still aware of its existence they do not recall its association with healing qualities.

Fuaran Bhiogair

Fuaran Bhìogair NB 347519

This spring is situated in a cleft in a rock at the shore at Bhìogair. It always contains bracing cold water. It was used to cure toothache and also to help relieve those suffering from mental illness.

Fuaran Bhinnisgro/Ghuinnisgro
NB 355483

This well is situated on the Barvas Moor to the west of the river, approximately a mile south west of the village. It is a large well - about a foot wide and about two feet in length, with yellow/brown sides. Beside it stands a lovely white stone.

According to Peter Macleod of Barvas, those suffering from diabetes or stomach pains used to come to it. People used to regurgitate what they had drunk from it, and this gave them relief. Its water was also used to relieve rheumatism.

Fuaran an Talaimh Mholaich
NB 305485

This spring is among the crofts, at Cnoc an Ois to the west of Arnol village. It was recognised as having qualities to relieve those suffering from stomach pain. The late Dr Ross used to give water from this well to those complaining of stomach pains.

Every Sunday, the young men of the village used to visit this well carrying a flask in their pocket.

Fuaran Buaile Dhòmhnaill NB 289486

This spring was situated in croft-land among the furrows of oats and barley, about 200 yards south of Teampall Eòin. It might have been the well used by those associated with that church in days gone by. It was in a hollow among the grass, and measured about three feet wide. A lively spring of water arose from its centre, and a film, resembling oil was to be seen on the surface of the water.

Water from this well was brought to those who were ill; sometimes to those who were patients in the Lewis Hospital. According to Aonghas Phàdraig from Bragar, its water was also used to cure toothache.

Round about 1980, it was completely destroyed by a JCB.

Fuaran Gharson NB 264485

This spring is to be found in a stony bay at Garson in Shawbost: the spring is in a cleft at the foot of the cliff and on the left as you descend. Often if there is a storm it fills up with pebbles.

People used to visit this well to improve their health. The *Ordnance Survey Word Book* describes it as: "Apparently a kind of spa."

Tobar 'ic Thòmais/Tobar Bhalabhair
NB 198446

This well is known by two names. It is situated in the moorland, to the east of the village of Geàrranan. It contains lime. Stories are still told of people visiting this well to get water for those who were ill. Bottles of water were brought to those who were ill in hospital. Accounts are given of how the water was brought to those on their deathbed: they craved for it.

It was said that if a cow excreted close to the well it would spring up in another location nearby.

Tobar Chiarain NB 185426

This well is down in Laimsiadar, to the east of a bend in the wall which runs across the neck of the headland. Martin Martin also describes it: "A well at Loch Carlvay, that never whitens linen, which hath often been tried by the inhabitants." (90).

Teampall Chiarain was situated closeby, and also Stighe Chiarain descending close to it.

It was said that people came and went on their knees at Càrn a' Bheannaich, which is close at hand, and that the priest used to bless them with water from Tobar Chiarain. They would then place their head on a stone and sleep after they had been thus blessed, and that this stone was a special stone.

MacPhail wrote in the *Oban Times* in 1898: "Anyone with a lingering disease was taken to Ciaran's shrine. Walked deiseil (sunwise) round the temple. Whatever the ailment, if he could be induced to sleep in the church he was sure to begin forthwith to improve." This is very similar to Martin Martin's account of Teampall Mholuaidh in Eòropaidh.

Tobar Chiarain NB 194428

Strangely this is a second well in Carloway named after Ciaran. This one is situated in croft land, and although it bears the name of a saint, no one has any recollection of whether people went there to seek a cure for illness.

Tobar Càrn an Dòbhrain NB 342207

This well can be found at Aird a' Chaolais to the north west of Cliacabhagh in the north of Calanais. It is situated in the moorland and it seems as though it is a well with water strong in iron. People used to visit it because of its healing properties; as was often the case they compared its water to the waters of Strathpeffer (An Tobar).

Fuaran Tràigh Theinis NB 117353

This spring is also called the toothache well. It is situated in a cleft measuring approximately one foot wide in the rock above the shore to the west of Stung close to Tràigh Theinis in Rif, Uig. Sometimes it is full of black seaweed, but once it is cleaned out, the water is beautifully clear. It is surrounded by lime.

Tradition has it that it had to be visited on an empty stomach first thing in the morning. The person had to be accompanied but no conversation had to take place either on the way there or back. Three mouthfuls had to be taken; the first two had to be spurted into the sea and the third one was swallowed.

Tobar a' Bheannachaidh NB 038378

This sacred well was close to Taigh a' Bheannaich, to the west of Aird, Uig. T.S. Muir makes reference to it, but there is no mention of it in oral tradition nowadays.

Fuaran an Dèididh NB 037334

This well can be found in Crabhlasta, at Creag Reithamul, near Port Bhasdair. It is in the cleft of a rock above the shore. It was visited to bring relief to those suffering from toothache.

Fuaran Bhaile na Cille NB 047338

In the cemetery there once was a church called Teampall Chrìosd; Martin Martin referred to it as 'St Christopher's chapel in Uge'. And TS Muir (1885) says of the spring: "At Uig, 8 miles north of Mealastadh, there is a well called Tobar Nec Cieres, but no remains of the ancient church which was dedicated to Saint Christopher." (40-41).

Fuaran Gheòdabrigh NB 542462

This spring can be found on the shore south of the pier in North Tolsta. Its water was used as a cure for sore eyes. Sufferers wiped their eyes with the water.

Tobar Chùisdein

Tobar Chùisdein NB 514337

It was Martin Martin's account which highlighted this well: "St Cowsten Church. The well there never boils meat of any kind though it be kept on the fire all day." (90).

This was somewhat similar to the account he gave of Tobar Chiarain in Laimsiadar.

The *OS Original Name Book* gave a lengthy account when the sappers visited on 30 April, 1876: "St Cowstan's Well. A spring of excellent water between Garrabost and the shore. The water gushes out beneath the bank with considerable force and falls into the sea. On the farm of Garrabost. In ancient times the well was held in great esteem. Tradition is that all manner of diseases used to be cured by placing the patient under the cliff where the water falls to the shore."

This was undoubtedly a sacred spot, with the church and the well close to one another, having a special place in the affection of the people.

Tobar na Claich Glais NB 5225335

This well is to be found on the moor south of Allt na Muilne in Garrabost. The well is marked by a stone. It was visited in order to get relief from stomach pain.

An Tràiseachadh NB 4433

This well is at the north end of Sandwick. People used to hear pipe music coming from it, and according to legend the fairies spirited away a girl who was on her way to the well.

Fuaran Shòbhal NB 348247

This well is above the road, north of Soval Lodge. This is a lively spring with a bottom of blue clay. The water is particularly cold, and would seem to contain sulphur. Travellers often visited it. Fortunately, one Finlay Maciver looks after, it cleaning and caring for it: it is a pity there are not more like him to take an interest in these sites.

Fuaran an Dèididh NB 415171

This well can be found in Calbost but only the name remains in people's memories. It is situated near the Tobar Mhòr. Another name for it was 'Fuaran a' Chapaill'. It has been filled to the top with stones for some unknown reason.

Fuaran an Dèididh NB 3915

This well is at Loch Fuaran an Dèididh in Grabhair. According to Murdo Matheson from Grabhair, people visited this well when they suffered particularly severe toothache.

~ *Harris* ~

Tobraichean Uamh Uladal NB 078132

It is Martin Martin who has the first complete description of these two wells, which are in a cave high up in the side of Gleann Uladal. He says: "The largest and best fortified (cave), by nature, is that in the hill Ulweal, in the middle of a high rock; the passage leading to it is so narrow, than only one can enter at a time … The cave is capacious enough for 50 men to lodge in: it hath two wells in it, one of which is excluded from dogs; for they say if a dog do but taste of the water, the well presently drieth up: and for this reason, all such as have occasion to lodge there, take care to tie their dogs, that they may not have access to the water. The other well is called the dogs-well, and is only drunk by them." (112).

According to tradition a monster called Ula stayed in this cave, until it was killed by Dos Mòr Mac a' Cheannaiche. Dos' Stone under which they are both said to be buried is at the head of Loch Resort.

Tobar na Slàinte NB 1809

It is said that this well is situated up on the old Cliseam road. Nobody nowadays is sure of the exact location.

Tobar Mhàraig

Martin Martin describes this well: "There is one remarkable fountain lately discovered near Marvag-houses, on the eastern coast, and has a large stone by it, which is sufficient to direct a stranger to it. The natives find by experience that it is very effectual for restoring lost appetite; all that drink of it become very soon hungry, though they have ate plentifully but an hour before: the truth of this was confirmed to me by those that were perfecly well, and also by those that were infirm; for it had the same effect on both." (112-112).

Tobar Amhainn Suidhe NB 0804

This is a small well, situated above the road at the west end of Amhainn Suidhe. Apparently the water was good for people; they saw it as a mineral well, with water similar to the well at Strathpeffer.

An Tobar Ruadh

An Tobar Ruadh   NF 020939

This well is situated at the north end of the burn close to a standing stone in the village of Borve.

It was said that water from this well would give a good appetite to those who drank from it and that the water had both health and curative qualities.

Martin Martin says of it: "There is a well in the heath, a mile east from the village of Borve; the natives say that they find it efficacious against colic, stitches, and gravel." (112).

Tobar Chè   NG 031992

This well is to be found on Taransay, close to Teampall Chè.

Tobar a' Ghobha   NG 134916

This well is on a croft at Leacan Lì. The water was used to relieve stomach cramp or headaches. It was said that An Gobha took water for the curing of illness from there either at dawn or at dusk; it is believed that An Gobha refers to the bard, Gobha na Hearadh.

Tobar Chuidinis NG 8709

This well is among the crofts at Cuidinis (Croft No 6). The water in this well was used to perpetuate good health; Dr MacNab from Leverburgh used to take bottles of water from it to give to those who were ill.

Tobar na Slàinte NG 021866

This well was in Leverburgh, across the bridge, on the south side of the road. It was good for restoring people's health. A high tide could fill it up but it would be clean again in three days' time.

Tobar na h-Annaid NF 975846

This well is on Cillegraigh, close to the cemetery, above Caolas Sgàire between the Island and Easaigh.

The site of Teampall na h-Annaid is nearby; 'annaid' denotes the site of an ancient church. The name occurs elsewhere in the Western Isles: in Suainebost, in Siadar a' Chladaich and in the Shiants.

~ *Uibhist a Tuath* ~

Tobar Leathad Ularaigh

This well is on the island of Berneray and close to Sgorr na Gruagaich. People believed that the gruagach or brownie liked to be close to water. The water from this well was considered to be the best on the Island.

Tobar Chaluim Chille

Tobar Chaluim Chille NF 873765

This one is up by Port nan Long south of Clachan. Beveridge says: "Fully half a mile to the south is an old well, now disused but still bearing the title of Tobar Chaluim Chille." (278). It tends to fill up with soil but every so often it is cleaned out.

Tobar Crò Naomh

This well was in Sanday. Carmichael (1900) says: "This one cannot be located, the extensive and once populous district being now almost uninhabited." (260).

Tobar nan Sagart/Tobar nan Cupan
NF 838787

This well is close to the graveyard at Aird a' Mhorain, and to the cross in the rock. Pochin Mould (1953) says: "Nearby (to the cross) there is said to be a well called the Well of the Priest or the Well of the Cups, but I did not satisfactorily identify it, though there certainly were several small springs close to the cross. The cups refer to a cup-marked stone." (140-141). The *Stornoway Gazette* (11/1/77) says: "The cross is 200 yards west of the burial ground. Some yards to the south east of the cross a holy well overflows onto the shingly beach. Local names for it are 'well of the priest' and 'well of the cross'.

Tobar Bhàlaigh

This one was in Pàirc nan Each. It was said that the water in this well had similar qualities to the water in the spa at Strathpeffer.

Tobar Mheithinis NF 712732

This well is situated by the shore out at Rubha Mheithinis, west of Baile Loch. It was known as a healing well. A lady from the area has a vague recollection that her brother on his death-bed requested a drink from this well.

Tobar Chuidhearaidh

Tobar Chuidhearaidh NF 809695

This well is situated to the east of Rathad na Comataidh on the south slope of Maireabhal.

People came to this well for a toothache cure, and they did not speak on the way there, until they had had a drink from the well. They would leave a gift or a coin and then they would kneel and recite the following verse:

> Tha mise a' fàgail dèideadh
> Lèireadh gus cnàimh mo chinn
> Anns an tobair nach tràigh a chaoidh,
> An ainm an Athar, A' Mhic 's an Spiorad Naoimh.

> I hereby leave the toothache
> Pain almost wasting my head
> In the well that will never dry,
> In the name of the Father, The Son and the Holy Ghost.

Carmichael (1900) refers to it as 'Tobar Chuidh-airidh', Tobar an Dèididh', 'Tobar na cnoidh', (well of the worm) and 'Tobar cnuimh fhiacail' ('well of the tooth worm, from a belief that toothache is caused by a worm in the tooth') (2, 11).

Tobar na Trianaid · NF 815602

This well is approximatly a quarter of a mile south west of Teampall na Trianaid in Càirinis. Beveridge (1900) writes: "Two hundred and fifty yards south-west of the twin chapels (Teampall na Trianaid and Teampall Clann Mhic a' Phiocair) is Tobar na Trianaid which in all probability served as the well in connection with them. This is lined with a wall, and although but recently disused is very shallow and of distinctly uninviting appearance." (288).

The *OS Name Book* says: "This name signifies The Trinity Well and is applied to the well situated about 12 chains to the South West of Teampall na Trianaid."

Alexander MacDonald from Càirinis used to say that people from South Uist came to this well on the day of Trinity, up to the 1840s. Somebody filled in the well since then: some of his sheep were being drowned there.

Tobar an Leighis NF 816603

This well was in Càirinis, north of Teampall na Trianaid and closer to the shore than to Cnoc na Trianaid. The well is now choked up with yellow iris.

~ *Benbecula* ~

Tobar an Dèididh   NF 873765

This well is situated close to Teampall Chaluim Chille. Close to it is a cairn of stones and each person who visited the well seeking a remedy for toothache placed a stone on the cairn.

An Gamhnach

An Gamhnach NF 826529

This well is out by the roadside, to the south east of Ruaidheabhal, opposite Loch Hearamal. People visited it and drank from it to improve their health; they brought a sprig of heather with them and left it at the well as an offering. Foxgloves grow round about the site.

Swire (1966) wrote: "But after his many days at sea St Torranan was very thirsty: finding no fresh water, he prayed to God for a spring and one at once broke out of the hillside where he stood. Torranan blessed it and when he had drunk his 'seven satisfactions' of its sweet water he gave it thanks and called the spring 'Gamhnach', Farrow Cow, and prayed that it might never dry up. Later, it became a place of pilgrimage and every pilgrim, having drunk, placed a 'choice green leaf" in it as thanks to the cow."(107).

~ *South Uist* ~

Tobar Ard a' Mhachair

This one was at Cròic, at the new graveyard. Bottles of water used to be taken from this well for medicinal purposes. It is said that this well disappeared under sand drift.

Tobar Crò Naomh

This well was in Druim Mòr. Carmichael (1900) refers to it: "A well at Drimore, in South Uist, is called 'Tobar Crò Naomh', Well of the Holy Heart. All who drank of its refreshing and curative waters placed a votive offering in the cairn beside the well." (260).

Tobar Beinn Ghòit

The well in Uisnis is situated between Beinn Ghòit and Beinn a Tuath, about a mile from the lighthouse. It was visited for health purposes, and money used to be left in it.

Tobar Easbaig Eòghainn NF 804402

This well is out on the moor at the foot of Beinn an Tairbeirt. It was a health spring. Easbaig Eòghainn used to rest here, and have a drink from the well. It is well-built with stone walls.

Tobar Aonghais Ruaidh

This well is between Corodal and Hecla. The inhabitants of Dramasdal used to go to it, and they used to place pennies in it.

Tobar Creag an Fhìon

This well is very close to Uamh a' Phrionnsa. Bonnie Prince Charlie drank from this well and praised its water, and called it Tobar Creag an Fhìon - and the name continued. Clear water was said to be a form of wine; Duncan Bàn MacIntyre mentioned "fìon Allt na h-Annaid," or "wine from the stream of Annaid."

This is the well which the *Ordnance Survey* calls Tobar a' Phrionnsa: "This name given to a spring well of very pure water, which lies at the northern base of Beinn Sgreadhan. The name arose from Prince Charles visiting it when on the island. It means Prince's Well."

Tobar Aird Mhaoil NF 718299

It was said that people drank out of this well when they were feeling unwell. It is situated on the northern shore of the headland. High tides fill it with stones and sand.

Tobar an Dèididh NF 7534

This well is in the village of Snaoiseabhal, and the local people still know of it.

Tobar an Donnain NF 730278

This one is in Cill Donnain on the croft belonging to Iain Dhòmhnaill 'Ic Iain, close to the site of Teampall Chill Donnain (NF 731282). People used to take water from this well 'for illness'. It is well-built and has a wooden lid, and the water was used as sacred water.

Tobar Thiobartain   NF 7415

"Tobar Thiobartain nam buadh,
I air iomall an Domhain Mhòir."
(Tiobartan Well of the virtues,
On the verge of the Great Domain).

This famous well was in Smercleit, 'seachd imrichean o rathad an rìgh'. According to tradition it was seven strips of land to the east of the road which goes along by the shore: nowadays it has disappeared into the machair land. Tiobar or tiobart means a well. So here we have the well of wells.

It was said locally that an old woman came to the well with a horse which had a squint, in order to cleanse the horse's eye with water from the well. Because of this the well lost its powers. It closed up from then onwards. Carmichael (1900) gives a good account:

"Tobar Thiobartan nam buadh
A chasgas gach falc is fual.
An eilean iomartach a' chuain
Am fìor iomall an domhainn mhòir.

The well of Tiobartan of virtues
To quell flood and gravel,
In remotest isle of the ocean,
On the very verge of the great domain."

According to tradition, the well of Tiobartan was famous in olden times, the pilgrims resorting to it from afar. Then a man brought his sick horse to it, and the spirit of the well fled, shrieking, and never returned. The well is in the machair, near the sea, and is now filled with drift sand. (286).

Tobar Adhratobhta NF 796200

This well is close to Cill Choinnich, north east of Loch Baghasdal. The stones from the church were used to make the sheep-fank and the fank is on the site of the church. The well itself is situated amongst whins. Oral tradition has it that fishermen visited the well on their way to and from fishing.

Tobar na Reulaig NF 783096

This well is on Eriskay. It is a fist-sized hole in a stone slab between Uamh na Lice Ruaidhe and Sloc Ruadh, west of Reulaig. The hole is eight inches deep and can hold a pint of rain water. Local fishermen used it regularly.

~ *Barra* ~

Tobar nan Ceann

Tradition has it that a battle was fought on the island of Fuideigh and that three soldiers or Norsemen were beheaded; their heads were thrown into this well.

It was from Nan MacKinnon of Vatersay that I first heard tales which made reference to human heads in connection with wells. Although she began by telling of Fuideigh and the Norsemen, she would always come back to Mòr nan Ceann. In these tales she would make reference to Tobar nan Ceann, Tobar a' Chinn and Tobar Mòr nan Ceann, but she did not know the exact whereabouts of the well itself.

She told one tale which said that Lady Macneil was herself Mòr nan Ceann and that she is buried on Eilean Bhuneasain beside Caibeal Moire nan Ceann or Cill Bhrianain. According to her, Mòr nan Ceann ordered three men to be beheaded, and she washed the heads in Tobar Bharra before they were buried and that Mòr's own son, Ruairidh was made chief of the clan.

But there existed different 'versions' (as she herself would say) of this tale: some of them very strange and complicated (see Ross, 1961, 1962). In each tale a well has pride of place, and three heads in a creel, and a head which spoke, and a head or heads which are placed in a well. It is certain that what we have here is part of ancient oral tradition, with wells and human heads in close association.

Tobar a' Dhùgain   NF 6702

This well is in Bealach a' Dhùgain past Dubharaidh at Baile na Creige, and across from a' Chrìochain. The well was blessed by Father Dermont Duggan, so that the Barra people could drink from it and have support and intercession from him.

Dermont Duggan was sent to Barra by St Vincent de Paul in 1650, as the people had been without a priest for nearly eighty years.

(The Reformation had taken place in 1560).

Tobar Bharra

Tobar Bharra NF 706075

This is one of the most famous wells in the Western Isles. It is situated near Cille Bharra, on the east side of the road. It is a lovely well with a sandy bottom and an attractive appearance with the water bursting forth in three springs. The well is steeped in tradition. It was said that it was St Barr himself who opened the well; that he put his stick three times into the ground and that the three springs arose, none of them having dried up from that day forth.

Tobar air Beinn Eòlagaraidh NF 702074

There is a well close to the top of Beinn Eòlagaraidh, and although its name is not known, it is the subject of a particular tradition, accounts of which have appeared in many history books as far back as the 1660s. This is called the tale of the cockles.

Boece's history of 1527 gives an account of cockles having been in a well in Mull. But it was not long until the tale appeared on Barra.

Of the early accounts, it is Dean Munro's account of 1594 which is the best known: "In the north end of this Countrey of Barray there is ane heich know. Upon the heid of this know thair is ane spring and fresh water well. This well trewlie springis up certane lile round quhyte things ... likst to the shape, figure and form on ame little Cockle as it appeirit to me." (73-74).

Another account, round about the same time (in MacFarlane, 1630) puts it thus: "Ther is one litle spring and fresh water running out of ane grein hill above the Church, which doeth flow into the sea. And there are springand there certane litill Cockles shells which they alleadge that the samen doth flow into the sea out of the Well and doeth grow in another place next the Church not the tenth part of ane myll from the Church of Barray called Killbarray." The story becomes a bit difficult to follow.

Some of the accounts place the well on the plain - maybe Tobar Bharra, as we know it. For example, an earlier account in 1600 in Skene states: "Item, in this Ile (Barraigh) is ane weill quhairin growis cockles, quihilk is at the fute of ane hill callit the Hill of Barra, twa mile fra the sea." Martin Martin himself visited Barra and went to Tobar Bharra: "And they say that the Well of Kilbar throws up embryoes of cockles, but I did not discern any in the rivulet, the air being at that time foggy." (158). Did he by any chance refer to the wrong well!

The tale is still told this century. Alasdair Alpin MacGregor (1929) was of the opinion that he had secured the answer: "The spring which is identified locally as being the one that threw up 'embryoes of cockles' is situated within thee or four yards of the summit of Ben Eoligarry. The water in it is charged with calcium carbonate, which is deposited on sand grains and similar objects, thus giving rise to the superstition that the water contained minute cockles." (276).

And MacGregor (1929) also says: "Apart from the Well of Kilbar, whence the cockles found in such immense quantities on the Tràigh Mhòr were supposed to have been carried down, the well of St Mary and the well of St Barr are the only sources of fresh water in this vicinity." (316). So, is Tobar Chille Bharra the one on Beinn Eòlagaraidh and is St Barr's well the one with the sandy grain deposits? But where is Tobar Mhoire, Well of St Mary, in this locality?

And there is another story about another well round about here, but there is no certainty as to which one. There is an account in MacFarlane (1630) which tells of an incident of which the MacNeil of Barra and an old man told and in which they believed: "There is also a spring of fresh water ... When appearance of wars were to be in the the Countrey of Barray that certaine drops of blood hath oftymes bein sein in this spring and fresh Water Well. Lykewise whenever appearance of peace wold be in the Countrie that certain little bits of Peitts would be seen."

Between the cockles and the blood, the tales which are told about the wells around Cille Bharra are as interesting as any that are told about wells anywhere.

Tobar Cùl Beinn na h-Oib NF 6902

This is a healing well, in the Dark Glen. People visited the well for health reasons. A lady from Buaile nam Bodach told of how a local man kept going to the well for healing purposes for as long as he could.

It can be seen on the *OS* map as 'mineral well'.

The road to it runs alongside Loch an Dùin, and it is about 500 yards from the main road; about 10 steps away on the south side of the road.

Tobar Chaluim Chille

Tobar Chaluim Chille NF 649996

This well is in Tangasdal near Loch Thangasdal, in a place called A' Bheirbh. This is a particularly attractive well, large with sandy surrounds: the water is particularly hard.

This is both a blessing and wishing well. Nan MacKinnon (Nan Eachainn Fhionnlaigh) from Vatersay recounted that if you required anything all you had to do was to go there and make a wish which would be fulfilled. People visited the well in order to receive a blessing, particularly before embarking on a journey - such as the herring girls. They came to it the Sunday before they left. Also couples who intended to marry but who could not afford to until the next season, came to it: they would come to the well on Sunday to make a vow of fidelity.

In past times when a lot of fisherman were coming into Barra, Brethren fishermen from Buckie came to the well every Sunday. The Barra fishermen themselves went there every Sunday to drink from it, in the hope of getting a better catch during the week. Martin Martin (1696) says: "There is another well not far from Tangstill, which the inhabitants say in a fertile year throws up many grains of barley in July and August." (157).

Tobar nam Buadh   NF 665979

This well is situated in the forecourt of Caisteal Chiosmul in Castlebay. It is highly unusual for a well to be situated on a sea rock, and this has meant that the castle has been a particularly good fortress. The water in this well was noted for having healing qualities for smallpox.

Tobar Chaluim Chille   NL 565833

This well is in Mingulay. It is close to Cill Chaluim Chille, with the water coming out of the rock. Nan MacKinnon (Nan Eachainn Fhionnlaigh) from Vatersay had this information.

Tobar Chaluim Chille

Tradition has it that this one was situated on Ceann Bharraigh, but there is no evidence of it now.

~ St Kilda ~

Tobar nam Buadh   NA 088003

This well is particularly noteworthy in the history of St Kilda because definite practices and oral tradition are connected with it. Martin Martin wrote: "In this isle there are plenty of excellent fountains or springs; that near the female warrior's house is reputed to be the best, the name of it, Toubir-nim-buey, importing no less than the well of qualities or virtues; it runneth from east to west, being sixty paces ascent above the sea: I drank of it twice, an English quart at each time; it is very clear, exceedingly cold, light, and diuretick; I was not able to hold my hands in it for above a few minutes, in regard of its coldness; the inhabitants of Harries find it effectual against windy-chollicks, gravel, head-aches; this well has a cover of stone." (414).

TS Muir depicts it as: "A low square-shaped massy stone building, with a stone roof, covers the spring, which, after forming a pool in the floor of the cell, runs down the russet slope like a thread of silver to join the stream in the valley." (65).

MacAulay (1764) tells of how the people gave pride of place to the well and of how they believed in its properties: "Some little time ago, a person long afflicted with a distemper, which had defeated the skill of all the people about him, took it in his head to go from Harris to St. Kilda, upon a sort of religious pilgrimage. His meaning was, to lay his grievance before the patron of this fountain." (94). Strangely no account is given as to whether this person achieved any satisfaction on account of the trip to the well.

But his account is nonetheless helpful: "It was once a fundamental article of faith in this isle, that the water here was a sovereign cure for a great variety of distempers, deafness particularly, and every nervous disease. Near the fountain stood an altar, on which the distressed votaries laid down their oblations. Before they could touch the sacred water, with any prospect of success, it was their constant practice to address the Genius of the place with supplication and prayer. No one approached him with empty hands. But the devotees were abundantly frugal: the offerings presented by them were the poorest acknowledgements that could be made to a superior Being, from whom they had either hopes or fears. Shells and pebbles, rags of linen or stuffs worn out, pins, needles, or rusty nails, were generally all the tribute that was paid; and sometimes, though rarely enough, copper coins of the smallest value. Very frequently the whole expense of sacrifice was no more than some one of the little common stones that happened to be in the Pilgrim's way." (95-96). Beside the well there is a stone which was used as an altar, and it was there that they left their offerings.

MacAulay concludes: "The Saint, Angel, or Deity, to whom the wonder working Tobernimbuadh pertained, is now an unknown Being, his name having been long ago buried in oblivion." (100-101).

As I stood day after day drinking from the clear water of Tobar nam Buadh in Gleann Mòr, close to the house of the Ban-àrmainn, I could not help but think of the many people who came there to drink, now without trace, and the writings which have given us such insight into the lives of these people.

Tobar a' Chlèirich

MacAulay (1764) says: "The second holy well at St. Kilda is below the village, and gushes out like a torrent from the face of a rock. At every full tide the sea overflows it, but how soon that ebbs away, nothing can be fresher or sweeter than the water. The natives call it Toberi Clerich." (99).

Tobar Childa

Much has also been written about this well, because many were of the opinion that it carried the same name as did the island itself. Martin wrote: "There is a large well near the town, called St. Kilder's Well; from which the island is supposed to derive its name; this water is not inferior to that above-mentioned (Tobar nam Buadh); it runneth to the south-east from the north-west." (414).

MacAulay (1764) wrote: "The third sacred fountain at St Kilda is near the heart of the village, and is of universal use in the community. The water of it is sweet, light and clear like crystal. The people give it the name of tobar Childa Chalda." It is thought by some that that the word 'childa' stems from the Norse word 'kelda' meaning 'a well'.

Tobar na Cille NA 098984

This well is beside the site of Teampall Bhrianain, close to Geodha Chille Bhrianain. According to oral tradition if the wind was not favourable for fishing, the fishermen would go to Tobar na Cille and each of them would stand astride the well for an instant, as a result of which the wind would become favourable.

Tobar na h-Oige

It was said that this well is situated in the face of a rock. Martin spoke of it thus: "There is a celebrated well issuing out of the face of a rock on the north-side of the east bay, called by the inhabitants and others, The Well of Youth, but is only accessible to the inhabitants, no stranger daring to climb the steep rock; the water of it is received as it falls, into the sea; it runs towards the south-east." (414). Although this well described by Martin is no longer to be seen, oral tradition tells of another well by the same name which appeared in another part of the island. One day a man, tired as could be, was descending Conochair with a sheep on a lead. He came upon a spring which he had never seen before. He drank from it and felt as young as a youth. He left the sheep at that spot, and ran down to the village to tell about the well. When he returned, there was no sign of sheep or well. It was said that if he had left a piece of iron at the well that neither the well nor the sheep would have disappeared. As happens naturally, the well of youth had evaded him!

Other wells are mentioned as being situated on St Kilda, although we have little information about them. One of these was Tobar Chonasdain, and

Martin wrote about that one: "There is another well half a mile of this (St. Kilder's Well), nam'd after one Conirdan, an hundred paces above the sea, and runneth from north-west towards the south-east, having a stone cover." (414). There is also mention of Tobar a' Mhinisteir, but the name itself is all that remains.

Bibliography

M. MacLeod Banks, 1937, British Calendar Customs: Scotland. Vol 1. William Glaisher for the Folk-lore Society.

George F Black, 1893, Scottish Charms and Amulets, PSAAS, 3, 433-526.

Alexander Carmichael, 1972, Carmina Gadelica. Scottish Academic Press.

Alexander Fraser, 1878(a), Ancient Wells in the North and Their Folk-Lore, Inverness Scientific Society & Field Club. Vol 1, 119-146; 1878(b) Northern Folk-Lore on Wells and Water, The Celtic Review, 3, 348-460.

Kenneth MacAulay, 1764, The History of St. Kilda. James Thin.

A.M. MacFarlane, 1927, Myths Associated with Mountains, Springs, and Lochs in the Highlands, TGSI, 34, 131-152.

Alasdair Alpin MacGregor, 1925, Behold the Hebrides! W&R Chambers; 1929, Summer Days Among the Western Isles. Nelson.

Alexander MacGregor, 1922, Highland Superstitions. Eneas MacKay.

James M. MacKinlay, 1893, Folklore of Scottish Lochs and Springs. William Hodge.

Finlay MacLeod, 1997, The Chapels in the Western Isles. Acair.

F. Marian McNeill, 1957, The Silver Bough: Scottish Folklore and Folk-belief. Vol 1. William MacLennan.

Malcolm MacPhail, 1898, Articles on Lewis Chapels. Oban Times.

Martin Martin, 1934, A Voyage to St. Kilda; A Description of the

Western Isles of Scotland. Eneas Mackay.

Arthur Mitchell, 1862, On Various Superstitions in the North-West Highlands and Islands of Scotland, Especially in Relation to Lunacy, PSAS, 4, 251-288, 1880, The Past in the Present. David Douglas.

Dean Monro, 1549, Western Isles of Scotland. (ed. R.W. Munro, 1961, Oliver and Boyd).

T.S. Muir, 1861, Characteristics of Old Church Architecture; 1885, Ecclesiological Notes on Some of the Islands of Scotland. David Douglas.

Thomas Pennant, 1774, A Tour in Scotland, and Voyages to the Hebrides; 1772. Chester.

Anne Ross, 1961, A Story from Vatersay, Scottish Studies, 5, 108-109; 1962, Severed Heads in Wells: an Aspect of Well Cult, Scottish Studies, 31-48; 1976, The Folklore of the Scottish Highlands. B.T. Batsford.

Royal Commission, 1928, Ancient and Historical Monuments of Scotland: The Outer Hebrides, Skye and the Small Isles. HMSO.

Otta S. Swire, 1966, The Outer Hebrides and their Legends. Oliver and Boyd.

J. Russel Walker, 1883, "Holy Wells" in Scotland, PSAS, 152-210.

Notes

Notes

Notes